D1123194

North American Mammals
Sea Otter

Jinny Johnson

Published by Smart Apple Media,
an imprint of Black Rabbit Books
P.O. Box 3263, Mankato, Minnesota, 56002
www.blackrabbitbooks.com

Printed in the United States of America,
at Corporate Graphics in North Mankato, Minnesota.

Designed by Hel James
Edited by Mary-Jane Wilkins

Library of Congress Cataloging-in-Publication Data

Johnson, Jinny, 1949-
 Sea otter / Jinny Johnson.
    p. cm. -- (North American mammals)
 Includes index.
 ISBN 978-1-62588-037-6
 1. Sea otter--North America--Juvenile literature. 2. Sea otter--
Behavior--North America--Juvenile literature. I. Title.
 QL737.C25J625 2014
 599.769'5--dc23
                            2013000065

Photo acknowledgements
t = top, b = bottom
title page and page 3 neelsky/Shutterstock; pages 4-5 Tom + Pat
Leeson/ardea.com; page 6 iStockphoto/Thinkstock; 7 bierchen/
Shutterstock; 8, 9 Doc White@naturepl.com; 10 Kim Worrell/
Shutterstock; 12-13 iStockphoto/Thinkstock; 14 Kirsten Wahlquist,
15 naturediver/both Shutterstock; 16 Francois Gohier/ardea.com;
17 Reika/Shutterstock; 18, 19 iStockphoto/Thinkstock;
20 worldswildlifewonders, 21 fred goldstein/both Shutterstock;
22 Menno Schaefer, 23 Ryan Richter/both Shutterstock
Cover Bettina Baumgartner/Shutterstock

DAD0509
052013
9 8 7 6 5 4 3 2 1

Contents

I am a sea otter.

I live in the northern Pacific Ocean.

Water Baby

I was born in the sea
and my mom held me on
her chest to keep me safe.

When I was about
six weeks old my
mom began to
teach me how
to swim and dive.

She showed me
how to find tasty
food to eat, too.

Strong Swimmer

Now I'm a really good swimmer and I spend nearly all my life in the sea.

I can walk on land, but not very well.

Look at me bobbing up and down in the water!

Deep Diver

I can hold my breath and stay under for several minutes while I hunt for food.

When I'm under water my ears and nostrils close off so I don't get water in them.

Flippers and Fur

My back feet are webbed and act like flippers to help me swim.

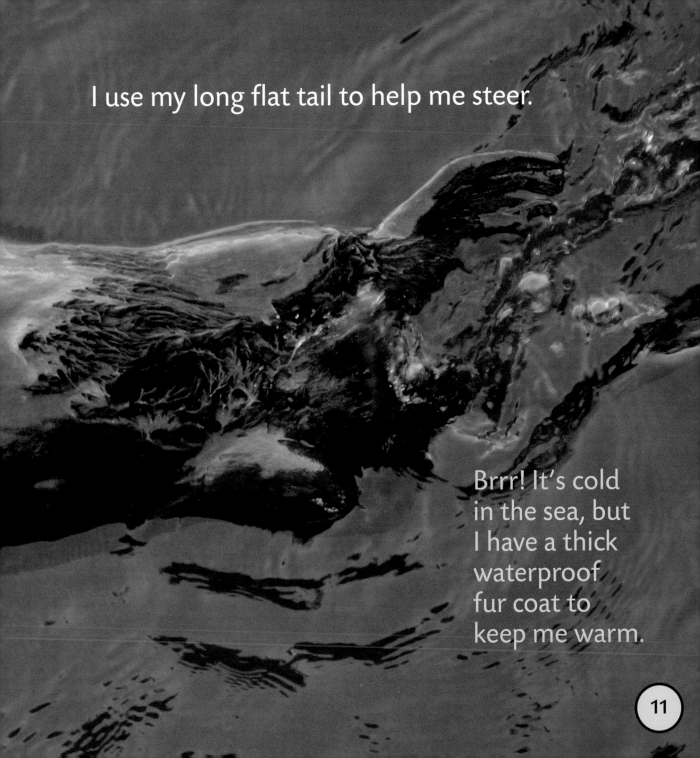

I use my long flat tail to help me steer.

Brrr! It's cold in the sea, but I have a thick waterproof fur coat to keep me warm.

11

Claws and Teeth

I have sharp claws on my front feet for grabbing hold of food.

In my mouth I have 32 teeth for biting prey and crushing their shells.

I have long whiskers, too. They are very sensitive and help me to search out food.

Finding Food

I dive down
to the seabed to
find things to eat.

sea urchin

I eat clams, mussels,
abalones, and crabs.
I like spiky sea urchins,
too and I can gobble
up as many as 50 of
them a day. Delicious!

Using Tools

Lots of the things I eat have a hard shell. When I'm hunting, I pick up a flat stone and tuck it under my arm.

When I come up to the surface, I lie on my back and put the stone on my chest. I bash my food on the stone to crack open the shell.

Then I can enjoy the tasty flesh inside.

abalone

Keeping Clean

When I've eaten, I always
groom my coat very carefully.

It takes a long time, but I have to keep my fur really clean so it stays waterproof.

Can you believe that some parts of my coat have up to a million hairs per square inch?

Staying Safe

A giant seaweed called kelp grows in the sea where I live. Before I go to sleep, I often wrap myself in kelp so I don't float out to sea.

Sometimes I hold paws with another sea otter, too.

Sea Otter Facts

The sea otter belongs to the weasel family—the picture, left, is of a weasel. The otter lives in water, but it is a mammal and must breathe air.

A sea otter needs to eat about 10 pounds (4 kg) of food a day. That's like you eating 40 hamburgers!

A full-grown sea otter can be four feet long, including its tail, and weigh 65 pounds (30 kg).

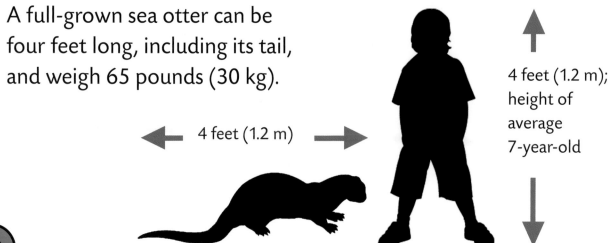

4 feet (1.2 m)

4 feet (1.2 m); height of average 7-year-old

Sea otters dive as deep as 250 feet (76 m) when they are looking for food. A 25-story building is about 250 feet (76 m) high.

Sea otters are an endangered species, which means that they are rare.

Useful Words

groom To care for and clean the fur.

mammal An animal that feeds its young with its own milk. Cats, dogs, and people are all mammals.

webbed A webbed foot has skin between the toes to help the animal swim.

Index

Web Link

Learn more about sea otters at
www.montereybayaquarium.org/animals